To: _____

From: _____

SUCCESS | BOOKS

200 Swisher Road
Lake Dallas, Texas 75065
U.S.A.
Toll Free: 800-752-2030
www.successmagazine.com

SUCCESS and SUCCESS Magazine are registered trademarks of R&L Publishing, Ltd.
SUCCESS Books is a trademark of R&L Publishing, Ltd.

Printed in the United States of America.

Cover and text design by Erica Jennings
Copy by J.M. Emmert

ISBN-13: 978-0-9790341-2-1
ISBN-10: 0-9790341-2-1

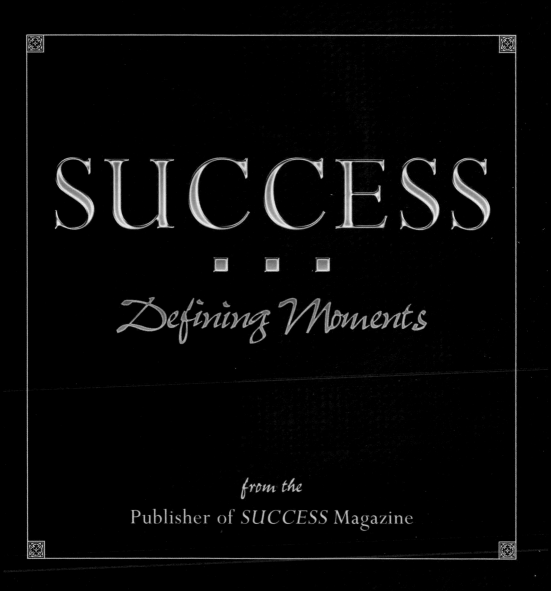

SUCCESS

■ ■ ■

Defining Moments

from the

Publisher of *SUCCESS* Magazine

Contents

■ ■ ■

Introduction

■ ■ ■

$\mathcal{W}$hat are the
moments that
change us,
that awaken
the slumbering
powers within,

*A*nd magically connect
us to the possibilities;
that flame our enthusiasm,
embolden our spirits,

*A*nd give our souls

the gift of flight;

$\mathcal{T}$hat increase the intensity

of our purpose,

To step out from the shadows
of uncertainty, to stand
against the winds and rain and
scorching sun, to refuse to be
beguiled into surrender?

When is the
moment that we set
our watch to the
hour of opportunity,

When we begin to
believe that the best
is still within us—

And yet to come?

A Potential Realized

■ ■ ■

$\mathcal{S}$uccess...

It is the quilt

sewn from the

patchwork of

our dreams:

the rich fibers

of loving family

and friends,

SUCCESS: *Defining Moments*

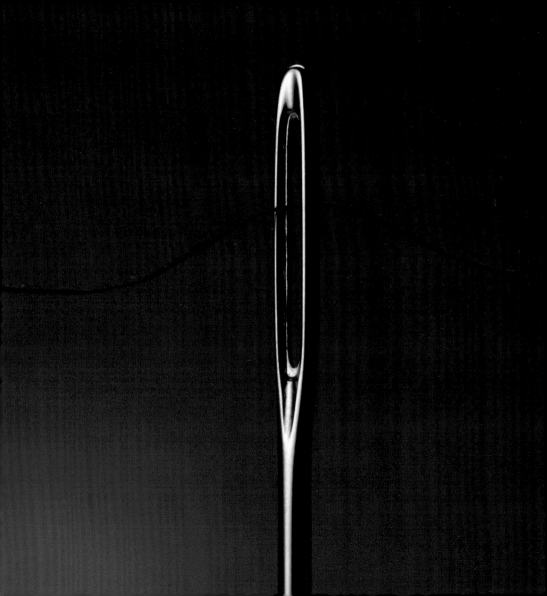

*T*he strong threads
of a healthy body,
soul, and spirit;

It is the handiwork
of the divine within
us, that comforts
throughout the
seasons of life;

$\mathcal{T}$he blanket
that wraps us up
in the warmth of
a life fulfilled.

Your Moment

■ ■ ■

What will the defining moment be, when you see that the golden opportunity you are seeking…

. . .is in yourself;

*I*t is not in your

environment;

it is not in luck

or chance, or the

help of others;

*I*t is in yourself alone.

The opportunity is now.

$\mathcal{M}$ake this your moment

Defining Moments

■ ■ ■

THOMAS EDISON

December 21, 1879

Demonstrates Incandescent Light Bulb

"If we did all the things we are capable of,
we would literally astound ourselves."

SIR EDMUND HILLARY

May 29, 1953

Reaches Summit of Mount Everest

"It is not the mountain we conquer, but ourselves."

SIR WINSTON CHURCHILL

May 10, 1940

Becomes Prime Minister of the United Kingdom

"Success consists of going from failure to failure without loss of enthusiasm."

MICHAEL JORDAN

June 21, 1991
Wins First NBA Championship

"*I*'ve missed more than 9,000 shots in my career. I've lost almost 300 games. Twenty-six times, I've been trusted to take the game-winning shot—and missed. I've failed over and over and over again in my life. And that is why I succeed."

RALPH WALDO EMERSON

September 1836

Publishes First Essay, "Nature"

"Men succeed when they realize that their failures are the preparation for their victories."

AMELIA EARHART

May 20, 1932

Flies Solo Across Atlantic Ocean

"The most difficult thing is the decision to act, the rest is merely tenacity. The fears are paper tigers. You can do anything you decide to do. You can act to change and control your life; and the procedure, the process is its own reward."

HELEN KELLER

March 3, 1887

Meets Teacher Annie Sullivan

"Character cannot be developed in ease and quiet. Only through the experience of trial and suffering can the soul be strengthened, ambition inspired, and success achieved."

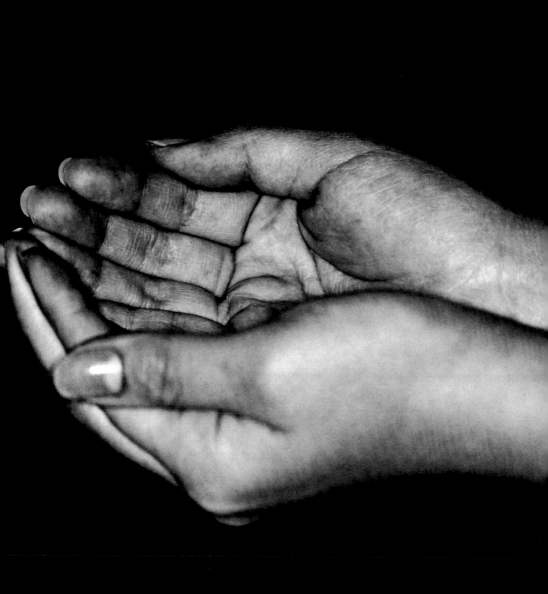

MARIO ANDRETTI

May 30, 1969

Wins Indianapolis 500

"*Desire is the key to motivation, but it's the determination and commitment to an unrelenting pursuit of your goal—a commitment to excellence—that will enable you to attain the success you seek.*"

OPRAH WINFREY

September 8, 1986

The Oprah Winfrey Show **Debuts**

"*D*o the one thing you think you cannot do. Fail at it. Try again. Do better the second time. The only people who never tumble are those who never mount the high wire. This is your moment. Own it."

BENJAMIN FRANKLIN

June 15, 1752

Conducts Famous Kite Experiment

"*W*ithout continual growth and progress, such words as improvement, achievement, and success have no meaning."

The Keys to Success

■ ■ ■

*W*hat are the stepping-stones
to achieving success?

Action

"Success is achieved and maintained by those who try and keep trying."

—W. Clement Stone,
Author of *The Success System That Never Fails*

Attitude

"*A* great attitude does much more than turn on the light in our worlds; it seems to magically connect us to all sorts of serendipitous opportunities that were somehow absent before we changed."

—Earl Nightingale, Author of *The Strangest Secret*

Choice

"*E*very life form seems to strive to its maximum except human beings. How tall will a tree grow? As tall as it possibly can. Human beings, on the other hand, have been given the dignity of choice. You can choose to be all or you can choose to be less. Why not stretch up to the full measure of the challenge and see what all you can do?"

—Jim Rohn, Author of *The Art of Exceptional Living*

Commitment

"Commitment is that turning point in your life when you seize the moment and convert it into an opportunity to alter your destiny."

—Denis Waitley, Author of *The Seeds of Greatness*

Courage

"Sometimes getting on the path to success and staying on it requires faith in the process—especially at the start. That makes you a pioneer. Pioneers don't know what's out there, but out there they go anyway. That's why being a pioneer takes such courage. Courage means to have a purpose and to have heart."

—Jeff Olson, Author of *The Slight Edge*

Enthusiasm

"Flaming enthusiasm,
backed up by horse sense and
persistence, is the quality that
most often makes for success."

—Dale Carnegie,
Author of *How to Win Friends and Influence People*

Goal Setting

"The victory of success is half won when one gains the habit of setting goals and achieving them. Even the most tedious chore will become endurable as you parade through each day convinced that every task, no matter how menial or boring, brings you closer to fulfilling your dreams."

—Og Mandino,
Author of *The Greatest Salesman in the World*

Gratitude

"The more you recognize and express gratitude for the things you have, the more things you will have to express gratitude for."

—Zig Ziglar,
Author of *See You at the Top*

Habits

"Whatever your present situation, I assure you that you are not your habits. You can replace old patterns of self-defeating behavior with new patterns, new habits of effectiveness, happiness, and trust-based relationships."

—Stephen Covey,
Author of *The 7 Habits of Highly Effective People*

Knowledge

"Knowledge is the raw material of production and value in this age. It used to be that the main difference between people in our society was between those who have more and those who have less. Today, however, the difference is between those who know more and those who know less."

—Brian Tracy, Author of *Success Mastery Academy*

Motivation

"*A* burning desire is the greatest motivator
of every human action. The desire for
success implants 'success consciousness'
which, in turn, creates a vigorous and
ever-increasing 'habit of success.'"

—Paul J. Meyer, Founder of Success Motivation Institute

Passion

"You were made for success—created for a unique and magnificent destiny! Dream the extraordinary! Pursue your passion with faith and tenacity and you will bring that destiny into reality."

—Chris Widener,
Author of *The Angel Inside*

Perseverance

"The strongest oak of the forest is not the one that is protected from the storm and hidden from the sun. It's the one that stands in the open where it is compelled to struggle for existence against the winds and rains and the scorching sun."

—Napoleon Hill,
Author of *Think and Grow Rich*

Positive Thinking

"Whenever a negative thought concerning your personal power comes to mind, deliberately voice a positive thought to cancel it out."

—Norman Vincent Peale,
Author of *The Power of Positive Thinking*

Tranquility

"The more tranquil a man becomes,
the greater his success, his influence,
and his power for good. He is like a
shade-giving tree in a thirsty land,
or a sheltering rock in a storm."

—James Allen, Author of *As a Man Thinketh*

A History of Success

■ ■ ■

ORISON SWETT MARDEN

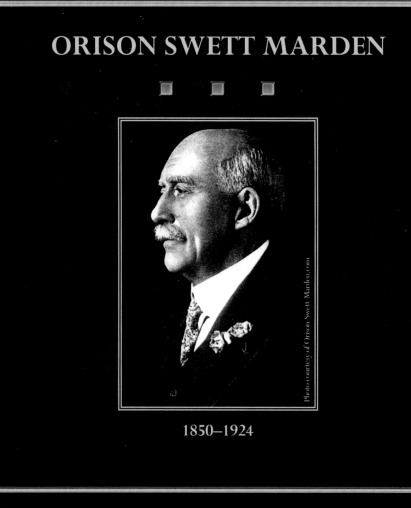

Photo courtesy of Orison Swett Marden.com

1850–1924

■ ■ ■

*O*rison Swett Marden was a 17-year-old New Hampshire farm boy toiling under abusive taskmasters in 1867. Orphaned at the age of seven, he was resigned to the fact that his life would never amount to anything. Then one day he discovered a book by Scotsman Samuel Smiles called *Self-Help*. It was the moment that changed his world, his fortunes, and helped lay the foundation for a life devoted to inspiring and encouraging others to reach their potential.

"*D*eep within man dwell those slumbering powers; powers that would astonish him, that he never dreamed of possessing; forces that would revolutionize his life if aroused and put into action."

—Orison Swett Marden

■ ■ ■

*M*arden became a leader of the New Thought Movement, the precursor to today's success movement. His masterpiece, *Pushing to the Front,* was a compilation of stories that described the extraordinary achievements everyday people made under the most extreme difficulties. The book became wildly popular and formed the basic philosophy for what would become *SUCCESS* magazine. Marden served as the editor of the magazine until his death in 1924.

"*The* greatest thing a man can do in this world is to make the most possible out of the stuff that has been given him. This is success, and there is no other."

—Orison Swett Marden

TO INSPIRE.
TO UPLIFT.

*T*o teach and to hold up models of success. That is the goal Marden had in mind when he launched *SUCCESS* magazine in 1891. For more than 100 years, it has been a source of inspiration, encouragement, and self-help to millions of men and women around the world who have aspired to be more and achieve more.

NAPOLEON HILL

Courtesy of the Napoleon Hill Foundation

1883-1970

*"*W*hatever the mind can conceive
and believe, the mind can achieve."*

SUCCESS: *Defining Moments*

■ ■ ■

*I*n 1908, Napoleon Hill was a 25-year-old reporter interviewing steel magnate Andrew Carnegie, who challenged him to compile the success secrets of the greatest achievers of the day——for the next 20 years of his life. Hill accepted the challenge, and spent years interviewing such men as Henry Ford, Thomas Edison, and Theodore Roosevelt. The result of his research led to the publication of *Law of Success,* which won worldwide acclaim. In 1937, he published his blockbuster, *Think and Grow Rich,* his philosophy of personal achievement that is considered one of the most motivational works of all time. Hill, an ardent admirer of Marden, revived *SUCCESS* magazine and served as its editor.

W. CLEMENT STONE

Courtesy of the W. Clement and Jessie V. Stone Foundation

1902–2002

"It takes less work to succeed than to fail."

■ ■ ■

*I*n 1937, W. Clement Stone, founder of Combined Insurance Company of America, was in debt. That's when he read *Think and Grow Rich* by Napoleon Hill. He became enthralled with the book and proceeded to apply its principles to his business. The result was an estimated personal fortune of more than $100 million. In 1952, Stone and Hill teamed up to bring Hill's 17 Principles of Success to the general public. The result of their partnership was the 1960 bestseller *Success Through a Positive Mental Attitude.* Two years later, Stone wrote *The Success System That Never Fails,* a guide that offered his insight into the accumulation of wealth and the creation of a healthy and enjoyable lifestyle. Stone served as publisher of *SUCCESS* magazine.

OG MANDINO

1923-1996

"I am here for a purpose and that purpose is to grow into a mountain, not shrink to a grain of sand.*"*

■ ■ ■

*O*g Mandino had been suffering from depression and on the brink of suicide when he picked up a copy of *Success Through a Positive Mental Attitude*. Inspired by the book, he sought work at Stone's Combined Insurance Company of America, subsequently working his way into management. In 1960, he was handpicked by Stone to become the new editor of *SUCCESS* magazine. An article he wrote on the legendary golfer Ben Hogan caught the eye of a New York publisher—and the rest was publishing history. *The Greatest Salesman in the World* was released 18 months later, and to this day remains one of the best-selling books on the philosophy of salesmanship.

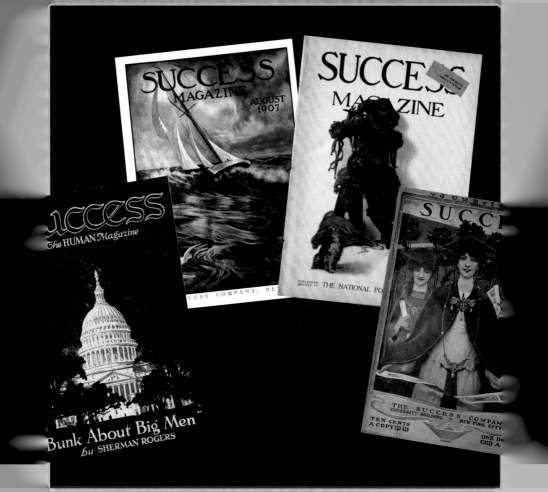

SUCCESS
MAGAZINE   AUGUST
1907

SUCCESS
MAGAZINE

PUBLISHED MONTHLY BY THE NATIONAL PO

CCESS COMPANY, NE

SUCCESS
The HUMAN Magazine

"Bunk About Big Men"
by SHERMAN ROGERS

SUCC

THE SUCCESS COMPANY
UNIVERSITY BUILDING
NEW YORK CITY

TEN CENTS
A COPY

ONE D
A

FROM THE PAGES OF *SUCCESS*

■ ■ ■

"*S*uccess is the ability to apply your physical and mental energies to one problem incessantly without growing weary."

—THOMAS EDISON, 1898

"*A*merica is the land of success…and an inspiration to inventors. Americans are more quickly appreciative of new inventions. Perseverance, practicability, and concentration [are] the chief factors of success."

—ALEXANDER GRAHAM BELL, 1899

FROM THE PAGES OF *SUCCESS*

■ ■ ■

"*I* do not think there is any other quality so essential to success of any kind as the quality of perseverance. It overcomes almost everything, even nature."

—JOHN D. ROCKEFELLER, 1900

"*S*uccess in life is largely a matter of coming up smiling at the proper moment; defeat is only a means to the ultimate end."

—F.W. WOOLWORTH, 1919

TODAY, THE TRADITION CONTINUES.

*M*arden's philosophy of uplifting, inspiring, and holding up models of success lives on in the all-new *SUCCESS* magazine.

*S*UCCESS offers you practical advice, ideas, tips, and training on leadership, goal setting, motivation, and much more. All in one beautifully designed, easy-to-read bimonthly magazine.

To subscribe, go to
www.successmagazine.com

Give the gift of
SUCCESS
to Family, Friends, and Colleagues!

— ❧ ❧ —

Order a *SUCCESS* magazine gift subscription for
those you care about and they will also receive
SUCCESS: Defining Moments.

For just $19.99, your recipient will receive
6 bimonthly issues of *SUCCESS* plus the beautiful
and inspirational *SUCCESS: Defining Moments* book.
Take advantage of this special opportunity and
share *SUCCESS* with everyone on your list!

Order now at
www.successmagazine.com/definingmoments
CALL 800-570-6414